An Insight into
Consumer Behavior for the
Successful Market Oriented Investors

By
Edebali Nurudeen

Table of Contents

Introduction

Marketing is an essential business discipline, and its contribution to the success of an organization is of immense value. An effective marketing result relied totally on how much understanding an investor has about the consumer of his or her products or services. The end result of marketing effort of every successful business is valued from the reaction of the consumer of his products or services. A good understanding of Consumer Behavior will show you how to take a strategic approach to the task. This book will cover helpful hints, deep information and strategic skill of analysis on consumer behavior, consumer decision process, market segmentation, getting to the consumers' head, consumer oriented strategic marketing etc. This book is an invaluable guide to improving your marketing performance and a companion for the students of knowledge.

1. Consumer Behavior

Consumer behavior refers to the study of how individuals, groups, or organizations make decisions and allocate resources to satisfy their needs and wants. It involves examining the psychological, social, and economic factors that influence consumer choices and actions.

1.1. Key Factors Influencing Consumer Behavior

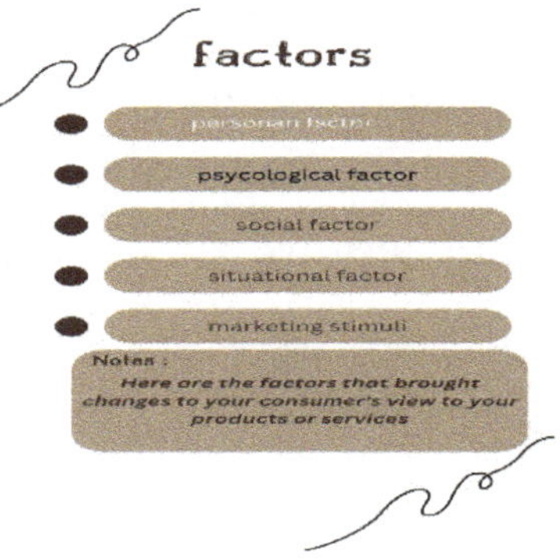

Several key factors influence consumer behavior:

Personal Factors: These include individual characteristics such as age, gender, income, occupation, lifestyle, personality traits, and values. Personal factors shape consumers' preferences, needs, and motivations, which in turn affect their buying behavior.

Psychological Factors: Psychological factors play a significant role in consumer behavior. Perception, motivation, learning, beliefs, attitudes, and emotions all influence how consumers perceive and respond to marketing stimuli. For example, an individual's perception of a product's quality or their emotional connection to a brand can impact their purchasing decisions.

Social Factors: Consumers are influenced by their social environment, including family, friends, peers, and cultural norms. Social factors can affect consumer behavior through socialization, reference groups, social class, and cultural values. For instance, individuals may buy certain products or brands to fit in with a particular social group or to express their cultural identity.

Situational Factors: The specific circumstances in which consumers find themselves can influence their buying decisions. Situational factors include the physical environment, time constraints, financial considerations, and the urgency or need for a product or service. For example, a consumer may be more likely to make impulsive purchases when they encounter a limited-time offer or when they are in a certain mood.

Marketing stimuli: Marketing efforts, such as advertising, promotions, product design, pricing, and distribution, can impact consumer behavior. Effective marketing strategies aim to understand and influence consumer decision-making processes.

Understanding consumer behavior helps businesses and marketers develop effective marketing strategies, tailor their products and services, identify target markets, and communicate their value proposition effectively. It also aids in predicting trends and consumer preferences, enabling companies to stay competitive in the market.

It's worth noting that consumer behavior is a complex field, and individual motivations and actions can vary significantly. Therefore, consumer behavior research often employs a combination of qualitative and quantitative methods to gain deeper insights into consumers' needs, desires, and decision-making processes.

1.2. Importance of Consumer Behavior

Consumer behavior plays a crucial role in various aspects of business and marketing. Understanding consumer behavior helps businesses make informed decisions and develop effective strategies to attract and retain customers. Here are some key reasons why consumer behavior is important:

Market Research: Consumer behavior analysis provides valuable insights into customers' needs, preferences, and purchasing patterns. By understanding why and how consumers make buying decisions, businesses can conduct market research to identify target markets, develop products or services that meet customer needs, and create effective marketing campaigns.

Product Development: Consumer behavior analysis helps businesses identify gaps in the market and develop new products or modify existing ones to better align with consumer preferences. By understanding consumer motivations, businesses can create innovative products that address their customers' desires and solve their problems, leading to higher customer satisfaction and loyalty.

Marketing Strategy: Consumer behavior insights inform marketing strategies and tactics. Businesses can tailor their marketing messages, promotional activities, and distribution channels based on consumer preferences, values, and buying behavior. This enables companies to effectively communicate the value of their products or services, differentiate themselves from competitors, and enhance customer engagement.

Pricing and Revenue Management: Consumer behavior analysis helps companies determine optimal pricing strategies. By understanding consumers' price sensitivity and willingness to pay, businesses can set prices that maximize profitability while remaining attractive to customers. Additionally, knowledge of consumer behavior aids in implementing revenue management techniques such as dynamic pricing and bundling, optimizing pricing structures based on customer segments and purchase patterns.

Customer Satisfaction and Retention: Understanding consumer behavior helps companies provide superior customer experiences. By aligning products, services, and customer interactions with consumer preferences, businesses can increase customer satisfaction, build trust, and foster long-term customer relationships. Satisfied customers are more likely to become brand advocates, providing positive word-of-mouth recommendations and contributing to business growth.

Competitive Advantage: Analyzing consumer behavior provides insights into competitors' strengths and weaknesses. By monitoring consumer preferences and behavior trends, businesses can identify market opportunities, anticipate competitors' actions, and differentiate themselves by offering unique value propositions. This competitive advantage allows businesses to attract and retain customers in a crowded marketplace.

Adaptation to Changing Markets: Consumer behavior analysis helps businesses adapt to evolving market conditions. As consumer preferences, technology, and societal factors change, understanding consumer behavior enables companies to stay ahead of trends and adjust their strategies and offerings accordingly. This flexibility and responsiveness are crucial for long-term business success.

In summary, consumer behavior is vital for businesses as it helps them understand customers' needs, preferences, and motivations. This knowledge empowers companies to make informed decisions regarding product development, marketing strategies, pricing, customer satisfaction, and staying competitive in dynamic markets. By focusing on consumer behavior, businesses can build stronger relationships with their target audience, increase customer loyalty, and drive growth.

1.3 Structural Aspect of Consumer

The structural aspect of consumer behavior refers to the underlying framework and components that influence how consumers make decisions and engage in purchasing activities. It involves understanding the various factors that shape consumer behavior, such as psychological, social, and cultural influences.

Structural Aspect of Consumer Behavior

Here are some *key elements* of the structural aspect of consumer behavior:

Individual Factors: These include personal characteristics, motivations, perceptions, attitudes, and learning processes that influence consumer behavior. For example, an individual's personality traits, values, and lifestyle can impact their purchasing decisions.

Social Factors: Consumers are influenced by their social environment, including family, friends, reference groups, and social norms. Social factors can affect consumer choices through word-of-mouth recommendations, social influence, and conformity.

Cultural Factors: Culture plays a significant role in shaping consumer behavior. Cultural values, beliefs, customs, and traditions influence how consumers perceive products and make purchasing decisions. Cultural factors vary across different societies and can impact consumer preferences, brand choices, and consumption patterns.

Situational Factors: The immediate circumstances or situation in which consumers find themselves can impact their buying behavior. Situational factors include factors like time constraints, physical surroundings, social setting, and the purpose or occasion for which a product is being purchased.

Decision-Making Process: The structural aspect of consumer behavior also encompasses the decision-making process consumers go through when making a purchase. This process typically involves several stages, including problem recognition, information search, evaluation of alternatives, purchase decision, and post-purchase evaluation.

Understanding the structural aspect of consumer behavior is essential for businesses and marketers as it helps them develop effective marketing strategies, design products, and create targeted advertising campaigns. By recognizing the underlying factors that influence consumer decision-making, businesses can tailor their offerings to meet customer needs and preferences more effectively.

Understanding
the structural
aspect of
consumer behavior

2. Consumer Decision Process

2.1. Decision

What is decision?

A *decision* is a mental process or action of selecting one option or course of action from among several alternatives. It involves choosing a particular course of action or making a judgment after considering various factors, options, and possible outcomes. Decision-making can range from simple everyday choices to complex and critical decisions with significant consequences.

Decisions are often influenced by personal preferences, values, beliefs, past experiences, available information, and the desired outcomes or goals. The process of decision-making typically involves gathering information, evaluating alternatives, weighing the pros and cons, assessing risks and benefits, considering potential consequences, and ultimately making a choice.

Decisions can be made individually or collectively, depending on the context and the individuals involved. They can also vary in terms of their level of complexity, significance, and the time frame in which they need to be made. Decision-making is an essential aspect of human cognition and plays a crucial role in various areas of life, such as personal matters, business, organizations, government, and public policy.

2.2 Consumer Decision Process

The consumer decision process, also known as the buyer decision process, refers to the steps or stages that individuals go through when making a purchase or consumer-related deWhile the specific steps may vary depending on the context and complexity of the purchase, the general consumer decision process typically involves the following stages:

Need Recognition: The decision-making process begins when a consumer recognizes a need or a problem to be solved. This can be triggered by internal factors (e.g., hunger, thirst, desire for entertainment) or external stimuli (e.g., advertisements, recommendations from friends).

Information Search: Once the need is identified, the consumer begins to search for information to gather knowledge about available options. This search can be internal (drawing from memory and personal experiences) or external (seeking information from various sources such as friends, family, reviews, advertisements, websites, or expert opinions).

Evaluation of Alternatives: After gathering relevant information, the consumer evaluates different options or alternatives based on specific criteria such as price, quality, features, brand reputation, and personal preferences. This evaluation process helps the consumer narrow down the choices to a manageable set.

Purchase Decision: In this stage, the consumer makes a decision to purchase a specific product or service. The decision may be influenced by various factors, including product availability, pricing, promotional offers, personal budget, and individual preferences.

Purchase: The consumer completes the transaction by buying the chosen product or service from a specific retailer or through a preferred channel, such as online or in-store.

Post-Purchase Evaluation: After making the purchase, the consumer assesses whether the product or service meets their expectations. They compare their actual experience with the anticipated benefits and satisfaction. If the product fulfills their expectations, it is likely to lead to customer satisfaction and repeat purchases. However, if there is a discrepancy between expectations and reality, the consumer may experience dissatisfaction and take actions such as returning the product or sharing negative feedback.

It is important to note that the consumer decision process is not always linear and can involve feedback loops. Additionally, factors like social influence, cultural norms, individual values, and previous experiences can also influence each stage of the decision-making process.

2.3 Types of Consumer Decision Making

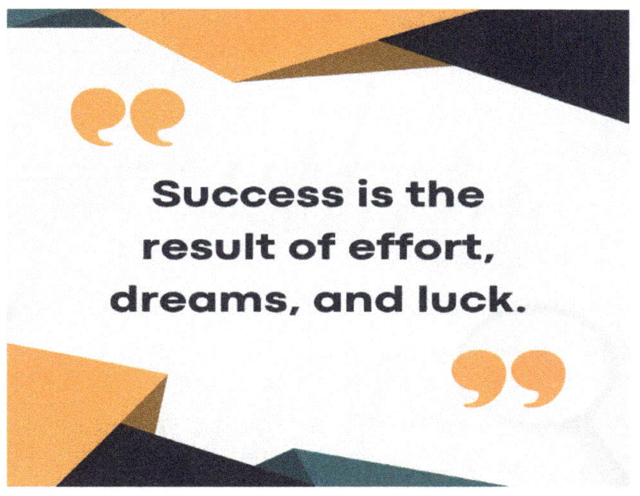

Consumer decision-making refers to the process through which individuals make choices and select products or services to fulfill their needs and desires. There are different types of consumer decision-making processes, including:

Routine response behavior: This type of decision making occurs when consumers have low involvement in the purchase decision and make choices quickly and habitually. It applies to frequently purchased, low-cost items like everyday groceries, toiletries, or snacks. Consumers often rely on prior experiences or brand loyalty to make these routine choices.

Limited decision making: This type of decision making involves a moderate level of involvement and effort. It occurs when consumers are faced with a purchase decision that is somewhat important but not overly significant. Consumers may spend some time researching and comparing options before making a decision. Examples include choosing a new smartphone or selecting a restaurant for a special occasion.

Extensive decision making: This type of decision making occurs when consumers face a high level of involvement and significance in the purchase decision. Consumers invest significant effort in gathering information, evaluating alternatives, and making choices. It typically happens when purchasing expensive, infrequently bought items such as a house, car, or major appliances.

Impulsive buying: Impulsive buying involves spontaneous and unplanned purchases made without extensive consideration or evaluation of alternatives. Consumers engage in impulsive buying when they are motivated by emotions, desires, or sudden impulses. Point-of-sale displays, limited-time offers, or attractive packaging can trigger impulsive buying behavior.

Emotional decision making: Emotional decision making refers to the process where emotions play a significant role in consumer choices. Consumers make decisions based on how they feel rather than relying solely on rational considerations. Emotional appeals in advertising, personal preferences, and the desire for self-expression can influence emotional decision making.

Rational decision making: Rational decision making involves a logical and systematic evaluation of alternatives based on objective criteria such as price, quality, features, or benefits. Consumers engage in this type of decision making when they consider the pros and cons of different options and make choices based on a thorough analysis of information.

It's important to note that these types of consumer decision-making processes are not mutually exclusive, and a consumer may employ different decision-making strategies depending on the specific product or situation.

2.4 Purchase Decision Process

The *purchase decision process* refers to the series of steps that a consumer goes through before making a purchase. This process typically involves several stages, which can vary in duration and complexity depending on the product or service being considered. Here are the general stages involved in the purchase decision process:

Recognition of a Need: The process begins when a consumer recognizes a need or a desire for a particular product or service. This need can arise from various factors, such as functional needs (e.g., a need for a new smartphone), psychological needs (e.g., a desire for status or self-expression), or social influences (e.g., peer recommendations).

Information Search: Once the need is recognized, the consumer engages in information search to gather relevant information about available options. This can involve seeking advice from friends, family, or colleagues, consulting online reviews and ratings, visiting stores, or researching websites, blogs, and social media platforms. The consumer aims to gather information that will help evaluate different alternatives.

Evaluation of Alternatives: In this stage, the consumer evaluates the available alternatives based on various criteria such as price, quality, features, brand reputation, and personal preferences. The consumer may develop a set of evaluative criteria or establish a hierarchy of importance for these criteria to compare different options.

Purchase Decision: After evaluating the alternatives, the consumer makes a purchase decision by selecting one product or service over the others. Factors influencing this decision can include price, availability, product features, brand loyalty, past experiences, and the consumer's financial situation.

Purchase: Once the purchase decision is made, the consumer proceeds to the actual purchase. This may involve buying the product online, visiting a physical store, or engaging in other purchasing methods.

Post-Purchase Evaluation: After the purchase, the consumer evaluates the chosen product or service based on their expectations and experiences. If the product meets or exceeds expectations, it leads to customer satisfaction. However, if the product falls short of expectations, it can result in dissatisfaction, potentially leading to returns, negative reviews, or decreased loyalty.

It's important to note that the purchase decision process is not always linear or predictable. Consumers can revisit certain stages, seek additional information, or engage in post-purchase behaviors like seeking support or sharing experiences with others.

Additionally, the level of involvement and complexity of the decision-making process can vary depending on the product's significance and the individual consumer's characteristics and preferences.

3. Market Segmentation Process

3.1 Market Segmentation

Market segmentation is the process of dividing a broad target market into smaller, more defined segments based on common characteristics, needs, preferences, or behaviors. It involves identifying groups of customers who share similar traits and creating distinct marketing strategies to effectively target each segment.

3.2 Factors for Market Segmentation

Segmentation can be based on various factors, including:

Demographic Segmentation: Dividing the market based on demographic variables such as age, gender, income, education, occupation, marital status, and ethnicity.

Geographic Segmentation: Segmenting the market by geographic location, such as country, region, city, or climate zone. This approach recognizes that consumer needs and preferences can vary based on their location.

Psychographic Segmentation: Dividing the market based on psychological and lifestyle characteristics, such as values, attitudes, interests, opinions, activities, and personality traits. This approach helps understand consumers' motivations, aspirations, and purchasing behaviors.

Behavioral Segmentation: Segmenting the market based on consumer behavior, such as usage patterns, benefits sought loyalty, purchase frequency, brand interactions, and response to marketing stimuli.

Socioeconomic Segmentation: Dividing the market based on socioeconomic factors, such as social class, income level, occupation, and education. This segmentation approach considers consumers' financial resources and social standing.

Technographic Segmentation: Segmenting the market based on consumers' technology adoption and usage patterns, such as device preferences, online behavior, social media usage, and digital skills.

B2B (Business-to-Business) Segmentation: In the context of business markets, segmentation can be based on industry type, company size, geographic location, purchasing process, or customer needs. This approach helps tailor marketing strategies to specific businesses and their requirements.

By segmenting the market, businesses can better understand their customers and design targeted marketing campaigns, develop tailored products or services, allocate resources efficiently, and enhance customer satisfaction. Effective market segmentation can lead to improved customer acquisition, retention, and overall business performance.

3.3 Target market positioning

Target market positioning refers to the strategic approach taken by a company to position its products or services in the minds of the target market. It involves creating a distinct and desirable image for the brand, product, or service, and communicating that image effectively to the target audience. Here are some common target markets positioning strategies:

Differentiation: This strategy focuses on highlighting unique features or benefits of a product or service that set it apart from competitors. By emphasizing what makes the offering different and better, companies can position themselves as leaders in their industry or niche.

Cost Leadership: This strategy revolves around offering products or services at lower prices than competitors while maintaining acceptable quality. By positioning themselves as the most affordable option, companies can attract price-sensitive customers and gain market share.

Niche Targeting: Some companies choose to focus on serving a specific segment of the market, known as a niche. By tailoring products or services to the unique needs and preferences of a niche audience, companies can position themselves as experts and gain a competitive advantage.

Quality and Premium Positioning: This strategy involves positioning a product or service as high-quality or premium in order to appeal to customers who are willing to pay a higher price for superior features, craftsmanship, or exclusivity. Companies often use branding, packaging, and marketing messages to create a perception of premium value.

Convenience and Accessibility: This positioning strategy focuses on offering products or services that are convenient and easily accessible to customers. By emphasizing factors such as ease of use, availability, and accessibility through various channels, companies can attract time-conscious or geographically diverse customers.

Sustainable or Ethical Positioning: With the growing emphasis on sustainability and ethical practices, some companies position their products or services as environmentally friendly, socially responsible, or aligned with certain ethical values. This can help attract customers who prioritize sustainability and ethical considerations in their purchasing decisions.

It's important for companies to conduct thorough market research and understand their target audience's needs, preferences, and perceptions in order to choose an effective positioning strategy. Successful positioning requires a clear understanding of the competitive landscape and a compelling value proposition that resonates with the target market.

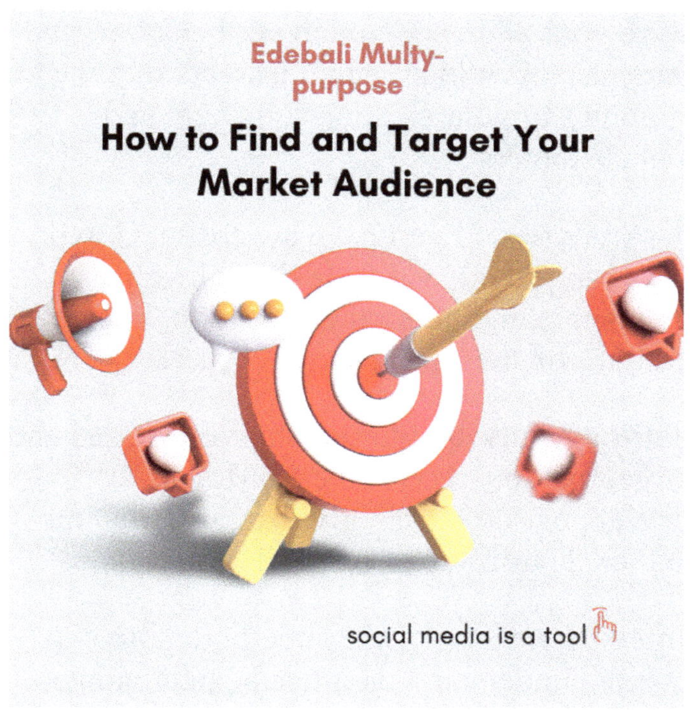

3.4 Target Market Tools

General tools and approaches to help identify a target market for a product or service.

Market Research Surveys: Create surveys to gather data from potential customers. Platforms like SurveyMonkey or Google Forms can help you collect information about demographics, preferences, and pain points.

Social Media Analytics: Utilize social media analytics tools such as Sprout Social or Hootsuite to analyze your audience's interests, behavior, and engagement. This will give you insights into the demographics of your existing followers and potential customers.

Google Analytics: If you have a website, Google Analytics can provide valuable data on your website visitors, including their location, interests, and behavior on the site.

Competitor Analysis: Study your competitors and their target markets. Tools like SEMrush, SimilarWeb, or Ahrefs can give you insights into their audience, traffic sources, and keywords.

Customer Interviews: Talk directly to potential customers to understand their needs, pain points, and preferences. This qualitative approach can provide valuable insights that data alone might not capture.

Persona Creation: Based on the data you gather, create buyer personas, which are fictional representations of your ideal customers. This will help you better understand and target your audience.

Google Trends: Use Google Trends to identify popular search terms and topics related to your product or service. This can give you an idea of what people are interested in and how search volume changes over time.

Industry Reports and Publications: Look for industry-specific reports, articles, and publications that might contain demographic data and market insights.

Focus Groups: Organize focus groups with representatives from your target market to gain deeper insights into their needs and preferences.

Ad Testing: If you plan to run ads, consider using A/B testing tools to test different messages and creative on small segments of your target audience to see what resonates best.

Remember that finding and understanding your target market is an ongoing process. Markets can evolve over time, so it's essential to stay up-to-date with the latest trends and be open to adapting your strategies as needed.

4. Consumer Research

Consumer research is a systematic process of gathering and analyzing information about consumers' preferences, behaviors, and attitudes towards products, services, brands, or marketing strategies. It involves studying consumer behavior and understanding their motivations, needs, and desires in order to make informed business decisions.

Consumer research typically involves various methods and techniques, such as surveys, interviews, focus groups, observations, and data analysis. These methods can provide valuable insights into consumers' buying habits, decision-making processes, satisfaction levels, and feedback on products or services.

The objectives of consumer research can vary depending on the specific goals of the business or organization conducting the research. However, some common objectives include:

Understanding consumer needs and preferences: Consumer research helps businesses identify what consumers want, their preferences, and the factors

that influence their purchasing decisions. This
information can guide product development,
marketing strategies, and brand positioning.

Market segmentation: Consumer research helps
divide the market into distinct segments based on
characteristics such as demographics,
psychographics, or behaviors. This segmentation
allows businesses to tailor their products, services,
and marketing efforts to specific consumer groups.

Brand perception and positioning: Consumer
research helps assess how consumers perceive a
brand, its image, and its reputation. It can identify
the strengths and weaknesses of a brand, as well as
opportunities for differentiation and positioning in
the market.

Product development and innovation: Consumer
research provides insights into consumer needs and
preferences, helping businesses create new
products or improve existing ones. It can uncover
unmet needs, identify areas for innovation, and test
product concepts or prototypes.

Marketing strategy evaluation: Consumer
research helps evaluate the effectiveness of
marketing campaigns, advertisements, pricing
strategies, and promotional activities. It can

provide feedback on the impact of marketing efforts and guide future strategies.

Customer satisfaction and loyalty: Consumer research helps measure customer satisfaction levels, identify areas for improvement, and understand factors influencing customer loyalty. This information can help businesses enhance customer experiences and build long-term relationships.

Overall, consumer research plays a crucial role in helping businesses understand their target audience, make informed decisions, and develop effective strategies to meet consumer needs and expectations.

4.1 Consumer research process

The consumer research process is a systematic approach used by businesses and marketers to gather information about consumers, their preferences, behaviors, and needs. This process helps organizations gain insights into their target audience, which they can use to develop effective marketing strategies, improve products or services, and enhance customer satisfaction. The consumer research process typically involves the following steps:

Identify the research objectives: Define the purpose and goals of the research. Determine what specific information or insights you want to gain about your target consumers.

Determine the research methodology: Choose the most appropriate research methodology based on your objectives. Common research methods include surveys, interviews, focus groups, observations, experiments, and data analysis.

Develop research instruments: Design the tools and instruments needed to collect data. This may include questionnaires, interview guides, observation checklists, or experimental protocols.

Sample selection: Determine the target population and select a representative sample. The sample should accurately reflect the characteristics of the broader population you want to study.

Data collection: Collect data using the chosen research methods. This may involve conducting surveys, interviews, or observations, or analyzing existing data sources such as sales figures or online analytics.

Data analysis: Analyze the collected data to extract meaningful insights. This may involve statistical techniques, qualitative analysis, or data mining approaches, depending on the nature of the data and research objectives.

Interpretation of findings: Interpret the results of the data analysis. Look for patterns, trends, and relationships in the data that can provide insights into consumer behavior, preferences, and needs.

Draw conclusions: Based on the interpreted findings, draw conclusions about your target consumers. Identify key insights and implications for your business or marketing strategy.

Report and presentation: Prepare a comprehensive report summarizing the research process, findings, and conclusions. Present the results to relevant stakeholders within the organization.

Action and implementation: Use the insights gained from the research to inform decision-making processes. Apply the findings to product development, marketing strategies, or customer experience enhancements.

It's important to note that the consumer research process is iterative, meaning that the steps may be revisited and refined as new insights emerge or additional research is conducted. The process helps businesses stay connected to their target consumers, understand their changing needs and preferences, and adapt their strategies accordingly.

4.2 Consumer Capability

Consumer capability refers to the ability of individuals or households to purchase goods and services in the market. It is a measure of their purchasing power and their capacity to participate in economic activities as consumers.

4.3 Factors for Consumer Capability

Consumer capability is influenced by several factors, including:

Income: The level of income directly affects a consumer's purchasing power. Higher income levels generally translate into greater consumer capability, as individuals or households have more money available to spend on goods and services.

Employment: The availability of stable and well-paying jobs is crucial for consumer capability. Employment opportunities and wage levels play a significant role in determining the purchasing power of individuals and their ability to meet their needs and desires as consumers.

Affordability: The cost of goods and services also affects consumer capability. When prices are high, consumers may find it challenging to afford certain products, reducing their capability to consume.

Access to credit: Consumer capability can be enhanced by access to credit, such as loans or credit cards. It allows consumers to make purchases even when they don't have immediate cash available. However, it's important for consumers to use credit responsibly to avoid falling into debt.

Education and financial literacy: Consumer capability can be influenced by the level of education and financial literacy of individuals. Knowledge about personal finance, budgeting, and understanding the market can empower consumers to make informed decisions and optimize their purchasing power.

Government policies: Government policies and regulations can impact consumer capability. Measures such as minimum wage laws, social welfare programs, and tax policies can directly affect the income and purchasing power of consumers.

Consumer capability is essential for a thriving economy as it drives demand for goods and services, which, in turn, stimulates production and economic growth. Policymakers and businesses often monitor consumer capability to understand market trends and make informed decisions regarding pricing, product development, and marketing strategies.

4.3 Consumer Marketing Channel

A *consumer marketing channel* refers to the various avenues and methods through which companies promote and sell their products or services directly to consumers. These channels are designed to reach and engage with the target audience, raise awareness about the brand, and ultimately drive sales. Here are some commonly used consumer marketing channels:

Advertising: This includes traditional forms such as television, radio, print media (newspapers, magazines), billboards, as well as digital advertising through platforms like social media, search engines, and display networks.

Digital Marketing: It encompasses a wide range of online strategies, including search engine optimization (SEO), pay-per-click (PPC) advertising, email marketing, content marketing, social media marketing, influencer marketing, and affiliate marketing.

Retail: Selling products through brick-and-mortar stores is a traditional marketing channel. Companies establish relationships with retailers and distributors to stock their products on shelves where consumers can purchase them directly.

E-commerce: With the rise of online shopping, e-commerce has become a crucial marketing channel. Companies can sell products through their own websites or utilize popular online marketplaces like Amazon, eBay, or Etsy.

Direct Mail: Companies may send promotional materials, catalogs, brochures, or coupons directly to consumers' mailboxes to generate interest and encourage purchases.

Events and Experiential Marketing: Companies organize events, trade shows, product launches, or experiential marketing campaigns to directly engage with consumers, showcase their products, and create memorable experiences.

Public Relations (PR): PR activities involve managing the company's public image and reputation through media relations, press releases, events, sponsorships, and other strategies aimed at creating positive exposure.

Word-of-Mouth: Encouraging satisfied customers to spread positive recommendations and referrals is a powerful marketing channel. Companies may utilize customer testimonials, online reviews, referral programs, or social media sharing to leverage word-of-mouth marketing.

Mobile Marketing: With the widespread use of smartphones, companies employ mobile marketing techniques such as mobile apps, SMS marketing, mobile advertising, and location-based marketing to reach consumers on their mobile devices.

Influencer Marketing: Collaborating with popular influencers and personalities on social media platforms to promote products and services is an effective consumer marketing channel, leveraging the influencers' large and engaged follower base.

It's worth noting that the choice of marketing channels depends on the target audience, product or service type, budget, and overall marketing strategy of the company.

4.4 Influence Consumer Behavior

What influence consumer behavior?

Consumer behavior is influenced by a wide range of factors, both internal and external. Here are some key influences on consumer behavior:

Personal factors: Personal factors include an individual's demographics (age, gender, income, education, and occupation), lifestyle, personality traits, and personal preferences. These factors shape consumers' attitudes, values, and beliefs, which in turn influence their purchasing decisions.

Social factors: Social factors encompass the influence of family, friends, reference groups, and society at large. Family members and close friends can significantly impact consumer choices through their advice, opinions, and shared experiences. Reference groups, such as professional associations or online communities, can also influence consumer behavior by setting norms and standards.

Cultural factors: Culture plays a crucial role in shaping consumer behavior. Cultural values, beliefs, customs, and traditions have a profound impact on what individuals perceive as desirable or acceptable. Marketers often need to consider cultural nuances to effectively target their products or services.

Psychological factors: Psychological factors encompass the cognitive and emotional aspects that influence consumer behavior. These include perception, motivation, learning, memory, attitudes, and emotions. Consumers' perceptions of products, their motivations for purchasing, and their past experiences with brands can all impact their decision-making process.

Economic factors: Economic factors, such as income, employment levels, and economic stability, influence consumer behavior. Disposable income affects consumers' purchasing power and their willingness to spend on goods and services. Economic conditions can shape consumer confidence and their willingness to make big-ticket purchases.

Marketing and advertising: Marketing and advertising activities significantly influence consumer behavior. Effective marketing campaigns, branding efforts, product positioning, and persuasive advertising messages can shape consumers' perceptions, generate interest, and influence their purchase decisions.

Technology and digital influence: The advent of technology and the widespread use of digital platforms have revolutionized consumer behavior. Online shopping, social media, product reviews, and influencers play a substantial role in shaping consumer choices. Technology enables consumers to gather information, compare products, and make purchases conveniently, influencing their decision-making process.

Environmental and Ethical Factors: Increasingly, consumers are considering environmental and ethical factors when making purchase decisions. Sustainability, corporate social responsibility, and ethical business practices can sway consumers who align their values with those of the brands they support.

It is important to note that these influences on consumer behavior can vary across different individuals and industries. Additionally, the relative importance of these factors may change over time as societal and economic conditions evolve.

4.5 Buying Center Overview

A buying center, also known as a purchasing center, refers to a group of individuals within an organization who are involved in the decision-making process for purchasing goods or services. The composition of a buying center can vary depending on the complexity and significance of the purchase.

Typically, a buying center includes the following roles:

Initiator: The person or group that recognizes the need for a particular product or service and starts the purchasing process.

Influencers: Individuals who can shape the purchasing decision by providing information, expertise, or opinions. They may include technical experts, department heads, or consultants.

Gatekeepers: People who control the flow of information to the buying center, such as receptionists or administrative assistants.

Deciders: The individuals responsible for making the final purchasing decision. They have the authority to approve or reject the purchase.

Buyers: The individuals who handle the actual procurement process, negotiate with suppliers, and finalize contracts.

Users: The end-users or employees who will utilize the purchased product or service.

Controllers: Individuals responsible for monitoring and managing the budget and financial aspects of the purchase.

It's important for businesses to identify and understand the members of the buying center to effectively engage with them and address their specific needs and concerns. Each member may have different priorities, preferences, and decision-making criteria, so tailoring communication and marketing strategies accordingly can increase the chances of successful sales and partnerships

5. Consumer Adoption Process

The consumer adoption process, also known as the consumer decision-making process or the buyer's journey, refers to the series of steps that individuals go through when considering and ultimately purchasing a product or service. These steps can vary depending on the complexity of the purchase and the individual's personal preferences, but generally, the consumer adoption process consists of the following stages:

Problem Recognition: The first stage occurs when a consumer recognizes a need or a problem that requires a solution. This need can arise from various factors, such as running out of a product, a desire for an upgrade, or exposure to new products or information.

Information Search: Once the need is identified, consumers start seeking information to evaluate possible solutions. They may gather information from various sources, including personal experiences, friends and family, online reviews, advertisements, product catalogs, and comparisons between different brands or models.

Evaluation of Alternatives: At this stage, consumers compare and evaluate different options available to fulfill their needs. They assess the features, benefits, and prices of various products or services, considering factors such as quality, reliability, brand reputation, customer reviews, and value for money.

Purchase Decision: After evaluating the alternatives, consumers make a decision to purchase a specific product or service. This decision is influenced by factors like personal preferences, price, availability, promotions, recommendations, and the overall perceived value of the offering.

Purchase: In this stage, consumers complete the transaction by actually buying the chosen product or service. The purchase may take place online, in a physical store, or through other channels depending on the consumer's preference and the nature of the product.

Post-Purchase Evaluation: After the purchase, consumers assess their satisfaction with the chosen product or service. They compare their expectations with the actual performance and quality of the offering. If the product meets or exceeds their expectations, they are likely to be satisfied and may become loyal customers. If there is a significant gap between expectations and reality, they may experience buyer's remorse and seek a return, refund, or exchange.

It is important to note that the consumer adoption process is not strictly linear, and individuals may enter or exit different stages depending on their specific circumstances. Additionally, external factors like marketing efforts, social influences, and cultural norms can significantly impact the consumer adoption process.

5.1 Customer Satisfaction

Customer satisfaction refers to the measurement of how satisfied customers are with a product, service, or overall experience provided by a business. It is a key metric that organizations use to evaluate their success in meeting customer expectations and building loyalty.

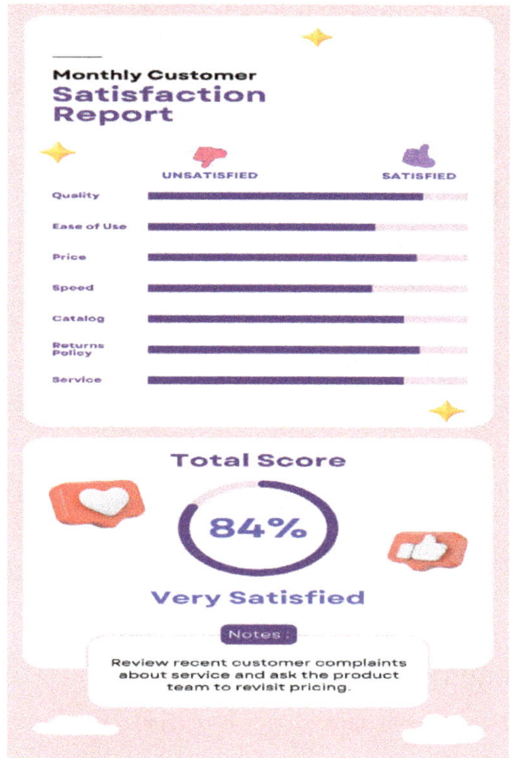

5.2 High Customer Satisfaction is Important for Several Reasons:

Customer loyalty: Satisfied customers are more likely to become repeat customers, providing ongoing business and potentially becoming brand advocates who refer others to the company.

Positive reputation: Satisfied customers are more likely to share their positive experiences with others, either through word-of-mouth or online reviews, which can enhance a company's reputation and attract new customers.

Increased sales: Satisfied customers are more likely to make additional purchases and spend more money with a company over time, leading to increased sales and revenue.

Competitive advantage: In today's competitive market, organizations that prioritize customer satisfaction can differentiate themselves from competitors, attracting and retaining customers in an increasingly crowded marketplace.

Measuring customer satisfaction can be done through various methods, including surveys, feedback forms, online reviews, and social media monitoring. Companies can also analyze customer complaints and support interactions to identify areas for improvement.

To improve customer satisfaction, businesses should focus on delivering high-quality products or services, providing excellent customer support, listening to customer feedback, personalizing experiences, and continually striving to exceed customer expectations. By doing so, companies can foster customer loyalty and create long-term success.

5.3 Total Customer Satisfaction Guide

Total customer satisfaction refers to the level of fulfillment or contentment experienced by customers after engaging with a product, service, or brand. It is a measure of how well a business meets or exceeds customer expectations and delivers value.

Achieving total customer satisfaction is crucial for businesses as it leads to customer loyalty, positive word-of-mouth recommendations, repeat purchases, and long-term profitability. Here are some key factors that contribute to total customer satisfaction:

Product/Service Quality: Customers expect products or services to meet or exceed their expectations in terms of performance, reliability, and durability. High-quality offerings that consistently deliver on their promises can lead to customer satisfaction.

Customer Service: Prompt, friendly, and efficient customer service plays a vital role in customer satisfaction. Resolving issues and addressing concerns in a timely manner can enhance the overall experience.

Personalization: Customers appreciate personalized experiences that cater to their individual needs and preferences. Customizing interactions, recommendations, and offers based on customer data can increase satisfaction.

Convenience and Ease of Use: Simplifying the buying process and making it convenient for customers to engage with a business can contribute to satisfaction. User-friendly interfaces, intuitive navigation, and hassle-free transactions are valued by customers.

Communication: Clear and effective communication is essential in building trust and ensuring customer satisfaction. Keeping customers informed about product updates, order status, or any changes can prevent misunderstandings and foster satisfaction.

Feedback and Continuous Improvement: Actively seeking customer feedback and using it to improve products, services, and processes demonstrates a commitment to customer satisfaction. Regularly incorporating customer input can lead to higher satisfaction levels over time.

Connection Emotional: Building an emotional connection with customers by creating positive experiences, resonating with their values, or fostering a sense of belonging can enhance satisfaction and loyalty.

It is important for businesses to consistently monitor and measure customer satisfaction through surveys, feedback mechanisms, and other means. This allows them to identify areas for improvement and take proactive steps to enhance the overall customer experience, ultimately leading to total customer satisfaction.

5.4 Monitoring Customer Satisfaction

Monitoring customer satisfaction is crucial for any business to ensure that customers are happy with their products or services. Here are some common methods and approaches to monitoring customer satisfaction:

Surveys: Conducting customer satisfaction surveys is a widely used method. Surveys can be distributed through various channels, including email, online forms, or even in-person interviews. The surveys can be structured with rating scales, multiple-choice questions, or open-ended questions to gather specific feedback.

Net Promoter Score (NPS): NPS is a metric that measures the likelihood of customers recommending your product or service to others. It typically involves asking customers a single question: "On a scale of 0-10, how likely are you to recommend our company to a friend or colleague?" Based on their responses, customers are categorized into three groups: promoters (9-10), passives (7-8), and detractors (0-6).

Customer feedback platforms: Utilize customer feedback platforms, such as online review websites or social media monitoring tools, to track and analyze customer comments, reviews, and mentions about your company. These platforms can provide valuable insights into customer sentiment and identify areas for improvement.

Customer interviews and focus groups: Conducting one-on-one interviews or organizing focus groups can offer deeper insights into customer satisfaction. These methods allow for in-depth conversations and discussions, allowing you to uncover specific pain points or areas where your business excels.

Customer support interactions: Monitor customer support interactions, such as phone calls, emails, or live chats, to gauge customer satisfaction. Analyzing customer support tickets and evaluating response times, resolution rates, and customer feedback can provide valuable insights into the customer experience.

Social media monitoring: Keep an eye on social media platforms to identify customer sentiment and engagement. Monitoring brand mentions, comments, and direct messages can help you address any concerns or issues promptly and engage with customers directly.

Online analytics: Analyze website analytics to understand customer behavior and satisfaction. Look at metrics like bounce rates, time spent on site, or conversion rates to assess how customers are interacting with your website and whether they are satisfied with the user experience.

Remember that *monitoring customer satisfaction* is just the first step. Once you gather feedback and insights, it's essential to take action and make improvements based on the findings. Continuously monitoring and addressing customer satisfaction will help build strong customer relationships and drive business growth.

6. Developing Marketing Strategy

Developing a marketing strategy requires careful planning and consideration of various factors. Here are some steps to guide you through the process:

Define your objectives: Start by clearly outlining what you want to achieve with your marketing strategy. Whether it's increasing brand awareness, driving sales, entering new markets, or launching a new product, having specific goals will help you develop a focused strategy.

Know your target audience: Identify your target market and understand their needs, preferences, and behavior. Create buyer personas to represent different segments of your audience and tailor your marketing messages and channels accordingly.

Conduct market research: Gather data and insights about your industry, competitors, and customers. This can include analyzing market trends, conducting surveys or focus groups, and studying competitor strategies. Use this information to identify opportunities and refine your marketing approach.

Develop your unique selling proposition (USP): Determine what sets your product or service apart from the competition. Your USP should highlight the key benefits and value you offer to customers. It will form the foundation of your messaging and positioning.

Choose your marketing channels: Based on your target audience and budget, select the most effective marketing channels to reach your customers. This can include digital channels like social media, email marketing, content marketing, search engine optimization (SEO), as well as traditional channels like print ads, direct mail, or television.

Create a compelling message: Craft a clear and compelling message that resonates with your target audience. Highlight the unique benefits of your product or service and communicate how it solves their problems or fulfills their needs. Ensure consistency in messaging across all marketing channels.

Set a budget: Allocate a budget for your marketing activities based on your objectives and available resources. Consider the costs associated with each channel and prioritize those that offer the highest return on investment (ROI).

Implement and monitor: Execute your marketing activities according to your plan. Track the performance of each channel and campaign using key performance indicators (KPIs) such as website traffic, conversion rates, sales, or customer engagement. Regularly analyze the results and make adjustments as needed.

Evaluate and optimize: Continuously assess the effectiveness of your marketing strategy and make data-driven decisions to optimize your approach. Identify what's working well and what can be improved, and iterate your strategy accordingly.

Stay adaptable: The marketing landscape is dynamic, so be prepared to adapt your strategy to new trends, technologies, and consumer behaviors. Stay updated on industry developments and be open to incorporating innovative marketing tactics.

Remember, developing an effective marketing strategy is an ongoing process. Regularly review and refine your approach to stay ahead of the competition and meet your business goals.

6.1 Consumer Behavior - Marketing Strategies

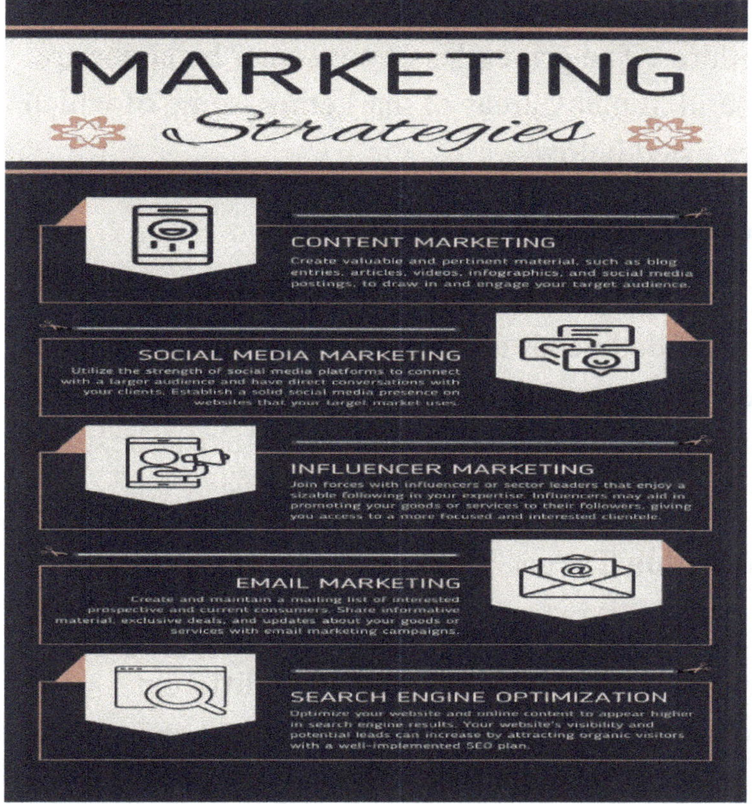

Marketing strategies and tactics are normally based on explicit and implicit beliefs about consumer behavior. Decisions based on explicit assumptions and sound theory and research are more likely to be successful than the decisions based solely on implicit intuition.

Knowledge of consumer behavior can be an important competitive advantage while formulating marketing strategies. It can greatly reduce the odds of bad decisions and market failures. The principles of consumer behavior are useful in many areas of marketing, some of which are listed below −

Analyzing Market Opportunity

Consumer behavior helps in identifying the unfulfilled needs and wants of consumers. This requires scanning the trends and conditions operating in the market area, customer's lifestyles, income levels and growing influences.

Selecting Target Market

The scanning and evaluating of market opportunities helps in identifying different consumer segments with different and exceptional wants and needs. Identifying these groups, learning how to make buying decisions enables the marketer to design products or services as per the requirements.

Example − Consumer studies show that many existing and potential shampoo users did not want to buy shampoo packs priced at Rs 60 or more. They would rather prefer a low price packet/sachet containing sufficient quantity for one or two washes. This resulted in companies introducing shampoo sachets at a minimal price which has provided unbelievable returns and the trick paid off wonderfully well.

6.2 Marketing-Mix Decisions

Once the unfulfilled needs and wants are identified, the marketer has to determine the precise mix of four P's, i.e., Product, Price, Place, and Promotion.

Product

A marketer needs to design products or services that would satisfy the unsatisfied needs or wants of consumers. Decisions taken for the product are related to size, shape, and features. The marketer also has to decide about packaging, important aspects of service, warranties, conditions, and accessories.

Example – Nestle first introduced Maggi noodles in masala and capsicum flavors. Subsequently, keeping consumer preferences in other regions in mind, the company introduced Garlic, Sambar, Atta Maggi, Soupy noodles, and other flavors.

Price

The second important component of marketing mix is price. Marketers must decide what price to be charged for a product or service, to stay competitive in a tough market. These decisions influence the flow of returns to the company.

Place

The next decision is related to the distribution channel, i.e., where and how to offer the products and services at the final stage. The following decisions are taken regarding the distribution mix —

Are the products to be sold through all the retail outlets or only through the selected ones?

Should the marketer use only the existing outlets that sell the competing brands? Or, should they indulge in new elite outlets selling only the marketer's brands?

Is the location of the retail outlets important from the customers' point of view?

Should the company think of direct marketing and selling?

Promotion

Promotion deals with building a relationship with the consumers through the channels of *Marketing Communication*. Some of the popular promotion techniques include advertising, personal selling, sales promotion, publicity, and direct marketing and selling.

The marketer has to decide which method would be most suitable to effectively reach the consumers. Should it be advertising alone or should it be combined with sales promotion techniques? The company has to know its target consumers, their location, their taste and preferences, which media do they have access to, lifestyles, etc.

Consumer behavior is a complex and multifaceted subject that influences the decisions and actions of individuals when it comes to purchasing goods and services. After analyzing various aspects of consumer behavior, we can draw several conclusions:

Changing Demographics: The demographics of consumers are continuously evolving, with shifts in age, ethnicity, income levels, and family structures. This diversity has led to varied preferences, needs, and consumption patterns among different consumer segments.

Digital Influence: The proliferation of digital technology has significantly impacted consumer behavior. The internet and social media platforms have transformed the way consumers research, evaluate, and purchase products. Online reviews, influencers, and personalized advertising play crucial roles in shaping consumer decisions.

Importance of Experience: Consumers increasingly prioritize experiences over mere ownership of products. They seek memorable and immersive experiences, both online and offline. This trend has fueled the growth of sectors such as travel and tourism, entertainment, and experiential retail.

Sustainability and Ethical Considerations: There is a growing awareness and concern among consumers about sustainability, social responsibility, and ethical practices. Consumers are more likely to support brands that demonstrate environmental consciousness, fair labor practices, and ethical sourcing.

Personalization and Customization: Consumers are seeking personalized products and services that cater to their unique preferences and needs. They value customization options that allow them to tailor offerings to their individual tastes, leading to the rise of personalized marketing and product offerings.

Convenience and Seamless Experiences: Convenience has become a significant factor in consumer decision-making. Consumers seek hassle-free and seamless experiences, such as fast delivery, easy returns, and user-friendly interfaces. The popularity of online shopping and the growth of delivery services highlight this trend.

Social Influence: Peer recommendations and social influence continue to impact consumer behavior significantly. Consumers rely on word-of-mouth recommendations, online reviews, and social media influencers to guide their purchasing decisions. Social proof and social validation play key roles in shaping consumer choices.

Emotional Factors: Consumer behavior is often driven by emotional factors rather than purely rational considerations. Emotions such as excitement, fear, happiness, and nostalgia can strongly influence purchase decisions. Brands that effectively tap into consumers' emotions can create stronger connections and brand loyalty.

Price Sensitivity: While consumers value quality and other factors, price remains a crucial consideration. Consumers are often price-sensitive and compare prices across different brands and platforms. Discounts, promotions, and price transparency play significant roles in consumer decision-making.

Continuous Evolution: Consumer behavior is not static; it evolves over time. External factors such as technological advancements, economic conditions, cultural shifts, and global events impact consumer behavior. Businesses need to stay attuned to these changes and adapt their strategies accordingly.

In conclusion, consumer behavior is a dynamic field influenced by various factors, including demographics, digital technology, experiences, sustainability, personalization, convenience, social influence, emotions, price sensitivity, and ongoing evolution. Understanding and effectively responding to these factors are critical for businesses to succeed in a rapidly changing marketplace.

If you have questions or if you need further help, please contact me through my email address below.

Yours sincerely,

Nurudeen Mustapha

manurudeen@gmail.com